6 50

"Art is a lie that makes us realize truth . . ."

Pablo Picasso

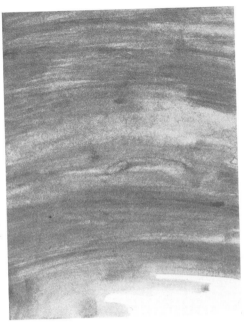

1. All gray . . .

2. A dark shape . . .

5. Some drippy lines . . .

6. Throw in some skinny crayon lines . . .

3.   Some dark, fat lines . . .

4.   Some fuzzy, light gray lines . . .

7.   A white dot and a wiggling of white lines . . .

8.   A daub of white, smudged out; a small black dot inside the big white dot . . .

TARA! We now have an example of . . .

The DOT, LINE and SHAPE CONNECTION

or HOW TO BE DRIVEN TO ABSTRACTION

Lee J. Ames

Doubleday & Company, Inc.
Garden City, New York   1982

FOR TOM AYLESWORTH

ACKNOWLEDGMENTS

The author and publisher are grateful for the permission to reproduce the following paintings:

Runner II by WILLI BAUMEISTER
Courtesy of Baumeister-Archiv, Stuttgart

Eight Red Rectangles by KASIMIR MALEVICH
Collection Stedelijk Museum, Amsterdam

Passage by PIERRE TAL COAT
Galerie Maeght, Paris

Vawdavitch by FRANZ KLINE
Courtesy: Sidney Janis Gallery, New York

Heroic Strokes of the Bow, 1938, by PAUL KLEE
Tempera on paper on cloth with gesso backing, 28-3/4 $\times$ 20-7/8″
Formerly Collection Nelson A. Rockefeller, Courtesy The Museum of Modern Art, New York

Agony, 1947, by ARSHILE GORKY
Oil on canvas, 40 $\times$ 50-1/2″
Collection, The Museum of Modern Art, New York
A. Conger Goodyear Fund

The Flesh Eaters by WILLIAM BAZIOTES
Estate of William Baziotes
Courtesy of Marlborough Gallery Inc., New York, New York

Shadows by JACKSON POLLOCK
Courtesy: Sidney Janis Gallery, New York

Broadway Boogie Woogie, 1942–43, by PIET MONDRIAN
Oil on canvas, 50 $\times$ 50″
Collection, The Museum of Modern Art, New York
Given anonymously

The author is also grateful for permission to reproduce photographs of the works of Robert Hasloecher, Mary Vaharian Anselmo, Gina Mascia, Lisa Thomson, Elke Brengard, Phyllis Sullivan, Josephine Glazebrook, Nancy and Richard Ackler, Trish Van Dina, Guy Hilbert, Jerry Fotinatos, Marian Mintzer, Jessica Loomer and Ed Sheridan ·

DESIGN: JOYCE WHEATMAN, LORRAINE ABRAMSON, MARIANNE BOSSHART

Library of Congress Cataloging in Publication Data
Ames, Lee J.   The dot, line and shape connection.
    1. Art, Abstract.   2. Art, Abstract—Technique.
I. Title.
N6494.A2A47   702′.8   AACR2
ISBN: 0-385-14402-4
Library of Congress Catalog Card Number 80–695
Printed in the United States of America   First Edition

What Is Abstract Art?

It is that art form which makes no attempt to create familiar or recognizable objects. The elements used range from geometric to amorphous (without definite form, shapeless).

Much as one can sometimes see "pictures" in cloud formations, you may see, in an abstract painting, something other than the painter may have intended. The colors or shapes may stir an old memory or awaken a forgotten mood, pleasant or otherwise. You may dislike or admire a childishly simple concept; you may admire or dislike an intricate complexity of color and form. Or you may feel confused and wonder how you're supposed to react.

This is similar to hearing a new or unfamiliar piece of music which may take many listenings to enjoy. As with music, a work of art may take time to appreciate. For good or for bad, let the new painting grow on you. Then if you have a choice of permitting yourself to express an opinion, remember, to *like* is better.

But, to repeat, the abstract artist does not attempt to create familiar or recognizable objects.

Before we get started, here's a selection of the work
of some of the masters! Linger here a while . . .

▼ 2

▲ 1

3 ▶

▼ 4

◀ 5

◄6

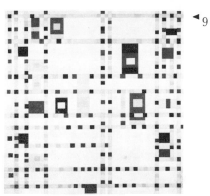

◄9

▲7 8►

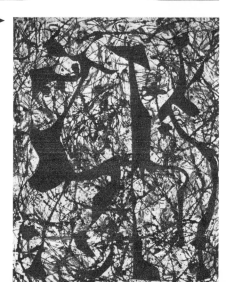

1. *Runner II*, 1934 WILLI BAUMEISTER

2. *Eight Red Rectangles* KASIMIR MALEVICH

3. *Passage*, 1957 PIERRE TAL COAT

4. *Vawdavitch*, 1955 FRANZ KLINE

5. *Heroic Strokes of the Bow*, 1938
   PAUL KLEE

6. *Agony*, 1947 ARSHILE GORKY

7. *The Flesh Eaters*, 1952
   WILLIAM BAZIOTES

8. *Shadows*, 1958 JACKSON POLLOCK

9. *Broadway Boogie Woogie*, 1942–43
   PIET MONDRIAN

9

There is much pleasure to be found in open-mindedly studying abstract art, and perhaps even more pleasure and satisfaction in its creation. In drawing or painting an abstraction, there are no limitations to what you may do. In such a totally free situation, however, you may find it difficult to know where to begin.

So! How do we start? Other than avoiding realistic, recognizable objects, there really should be no rules for creating an abstract work. But, for the purpose of getting under way, we will use only dots, lines and/or shapes in blacks or whites or grays.

When you think about it, a dot is really a small shape or a shape is really a large dot or a line is a long dot, etc. Still, for starters, let's think in terms of dots, lines and shapes.

There are many kinds of dots.

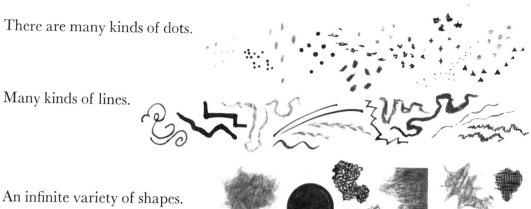

Many kinds of lines.

An infinite variety of shapes.

These can be light or dark or textured, smooth or rough, hard-edged or fuzzy, strong or faint or fading.

And they can repeat themselves in sequence, in reverse, in similarity.

A bunch of dots can become a line.

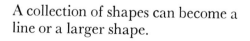

A cluster of dots may become a shape.

A crowd of lines may become a shape.

A collection of shapes can become a line or a larger shape.

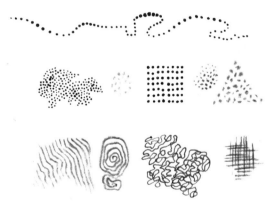

Here are some arrangements with dots.
Spend some time studying each one. Get
a sketch pad. See what interesting arrangements
you can come up with.

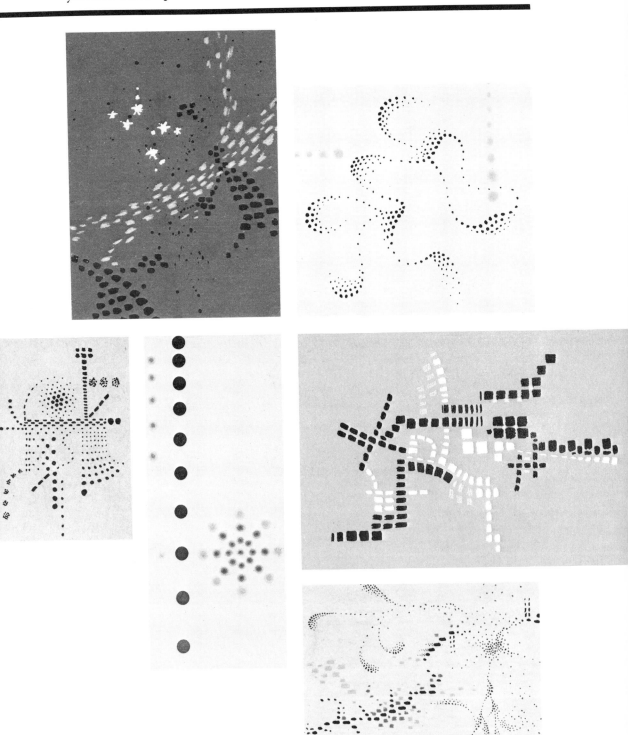

Now, some arrangements with lines.
Spend an hour and see what variations
you can create.

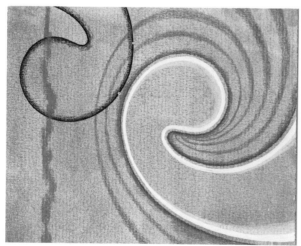
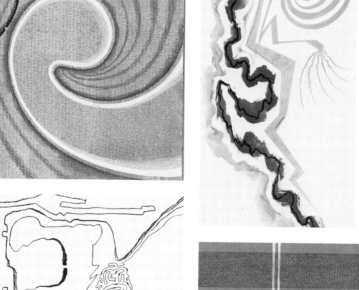
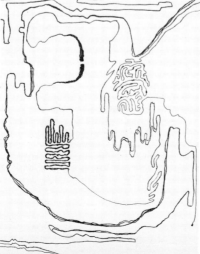
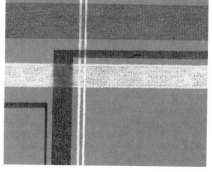

Try the same thing with shapes.
What new concepts can you come up with?

Exercise Time!

The next six pages contain combinations of:

1. Dots and lines
2. Dots and shapes
3. Lines and shapes

After studying these, try some combinations of your own. How many new relationships can you invent? How many interesting new designs can you arrange? Invest a few hours . . .

This is a discipline to help you develop your own unique design sense and skill, a practice well worth continuing as long as you remain interested in the creative arts.

Here are some experiments with dots and lines.

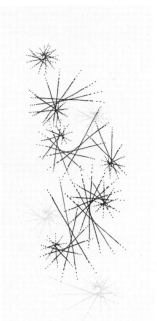

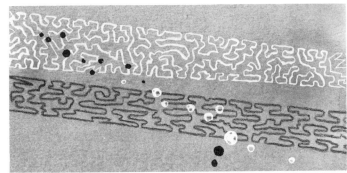

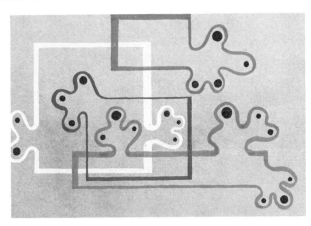

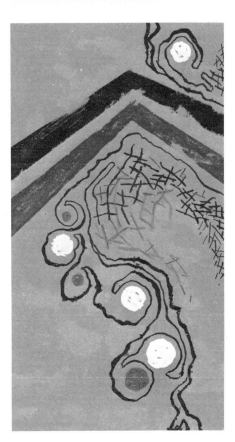

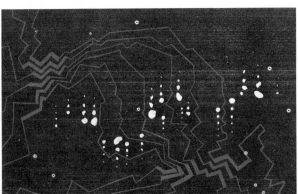

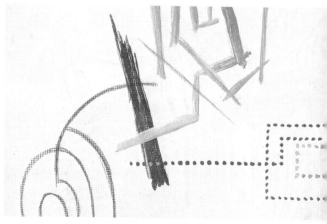

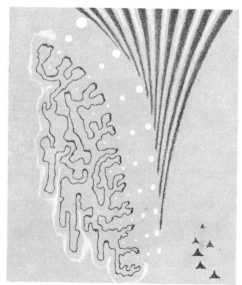

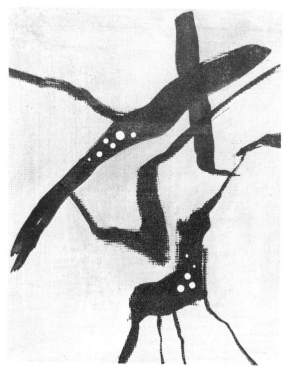

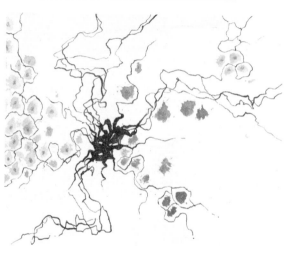

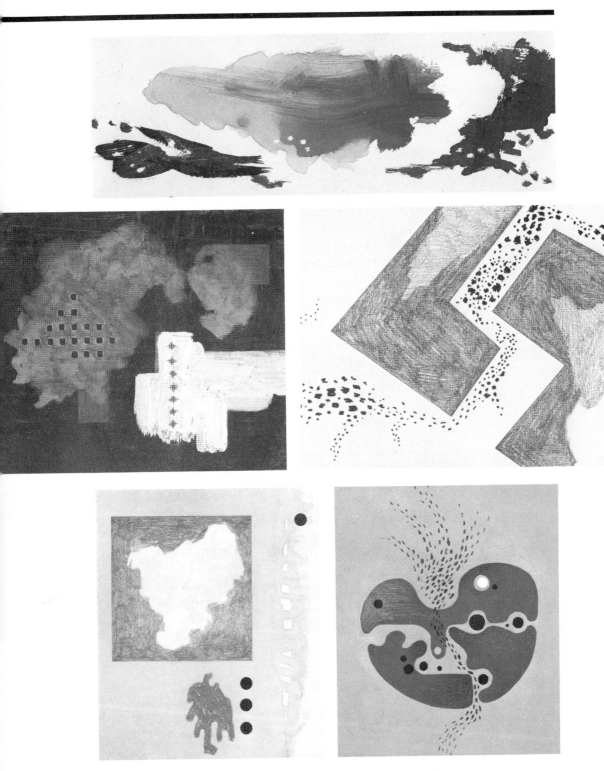

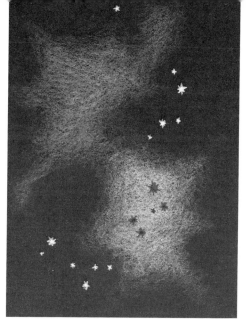

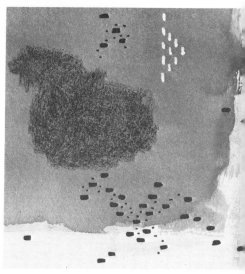

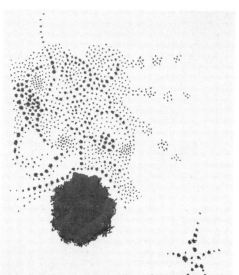

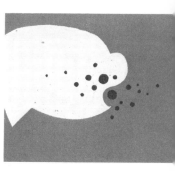

. . . lines and shapes.

 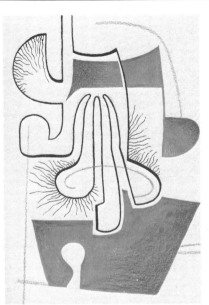 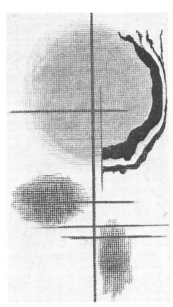

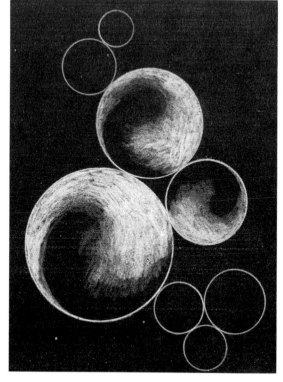

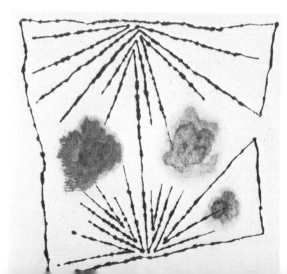

And Now, All Three!
What happens when you juggle dots, lines and shapes?

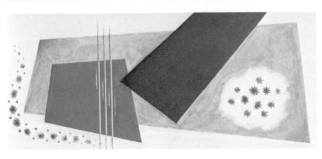
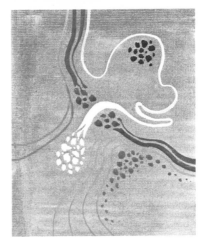
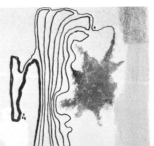

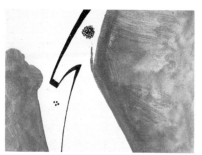

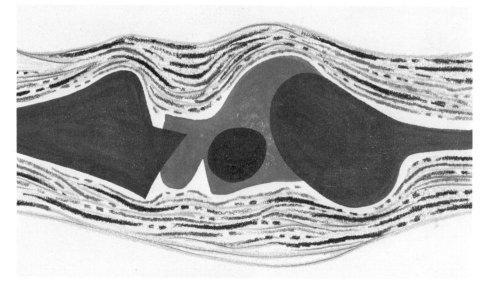

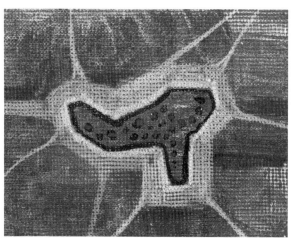

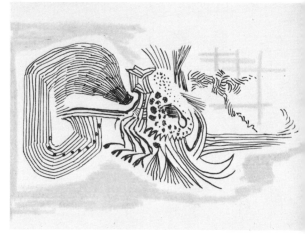

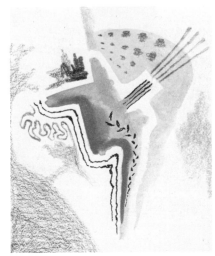

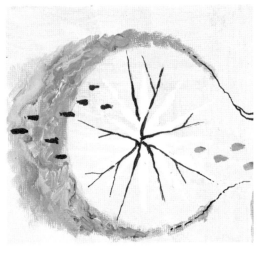

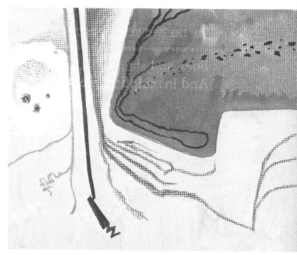

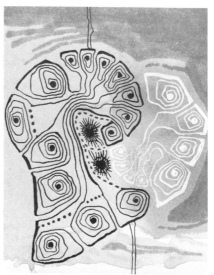

A New Dimension!

So far we've applied pencil, ink or paint to flat, two-dimensional
surfaces. Now let's sculpt, let's go three-dimensional. Instead of dots,
lines and shapes, let's work with tiny things, long things and big things.
And in sculpting, we can add a fourth element—flat things.

Some tiny things.

Some long things.

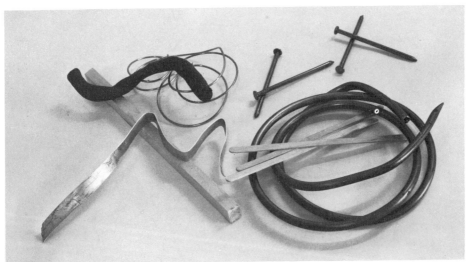

Some big things.

Some flat things.

Now . . . getting it all together, here are some possibilities.
What can you come up with?

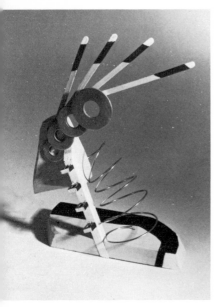

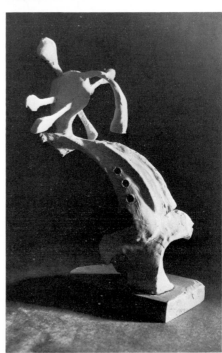

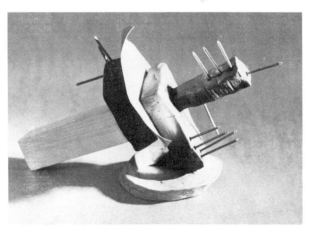

In creating an abstract photograph, avoid easily recognizable subject matter within the final picture area. Seek out arrangements of dots, lines and/or shapes (or tiny things, long things, flat things and/or big things). Don't hesitate to crop or combine prints or to add paint or ink. Consider the camera another tool to help you organize and express *your* concepts. Remember, your purpose is to come up with something that pleases *you*. This is *your* improvisation.

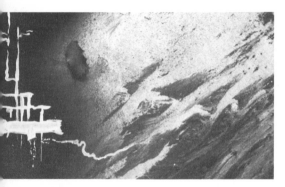

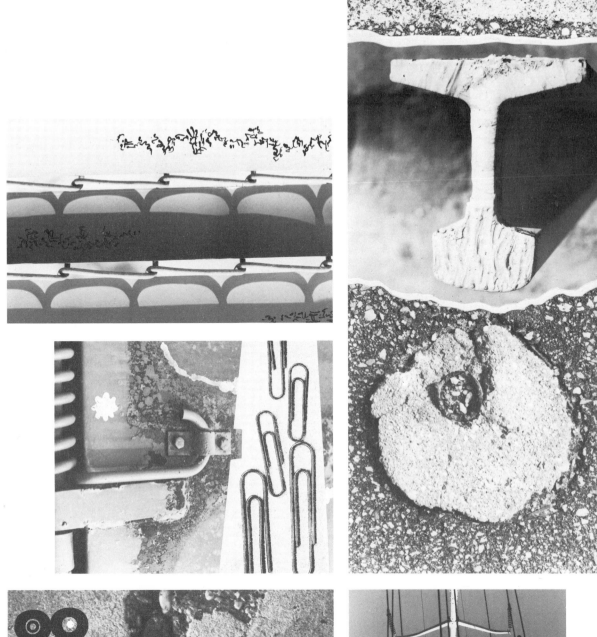

Did you ever try to "not think at all"? Impossible! If one is conscious, aware, there are thoughts in one's mind. Similarly, it is very difficult, if not impossible, to see anything as being purely abstract. At some level of awareness, an abstract image reminds us of some recognizable reality.

It is equally difficult to create an abstraction that is not rooted in a "real" concept. The ball-like round shape, the sharp angle, the hard edge etc. Then why not *use* this approach. Start with something recognizable as your inspiration and modify it into a satisfying abstraction.

Here are some results:

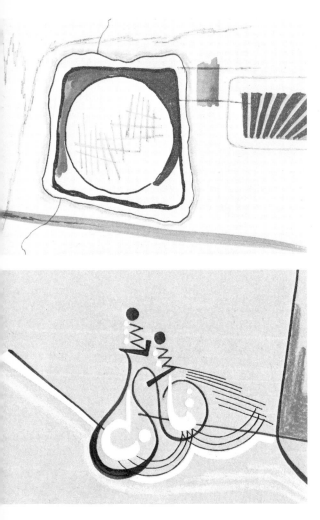

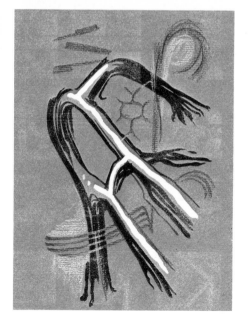

For the sources from which these were developed, turn to the next page.

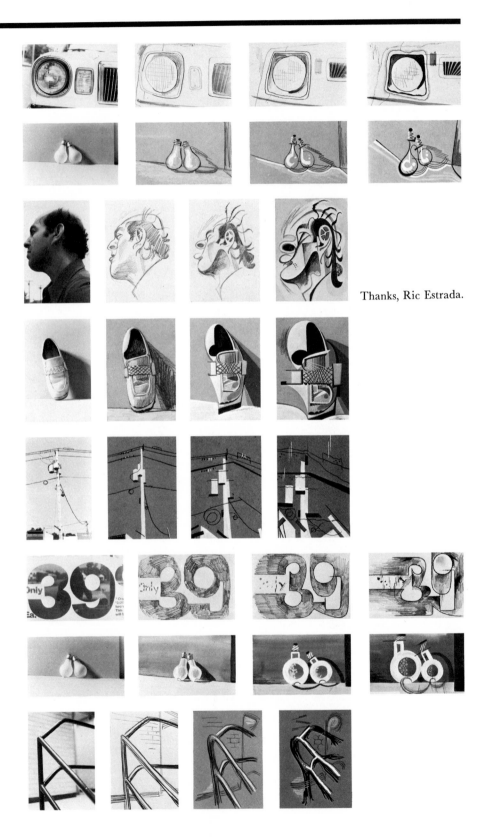

Thanks, Ric Estrada.

The Color Connection,
or The Use of Hues—Some Views and Clues

So far we've only dealt with blacks, whites and grays. It's time to add color. Don't be intimidated. The use of color, its combinations, intensities and arrangements are matters of very personal choice. Experiment, convey *your* moods and *your* color improvisations. 👣

However, this once it may be worthwhile trying an exercise our art teacher Miss Johnson gave us in school in 1935. The two patterns below were designed to be copied slowly and carefully in your choice of medium—gouache, tempera, watercolor, oil or acrylic. Copy as faithfully, as accurately, as you are capable of doing. Similar exercises in Miss Johnson's class impressed me that many years ago—and since —with the wonder of color, its subtlety and its potency.

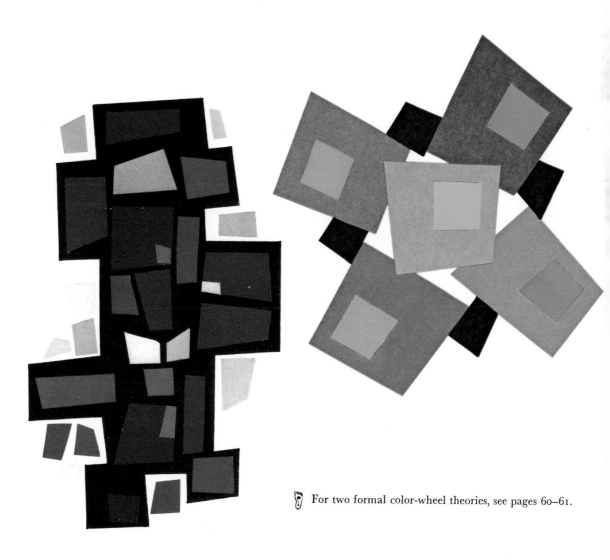

👣 For two formal color-wheel theories, see pages 60–61.

Plus Color!

To dots, lines and shapes, by themselves or in combinations, add color. Try it!
To little things, long things, big things and flat things add color!
In photography, think color, make use of color!

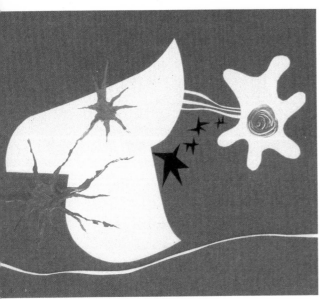

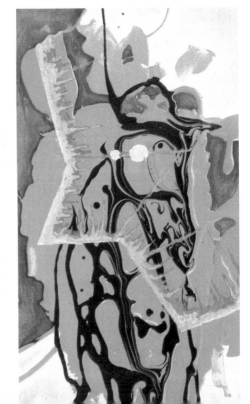

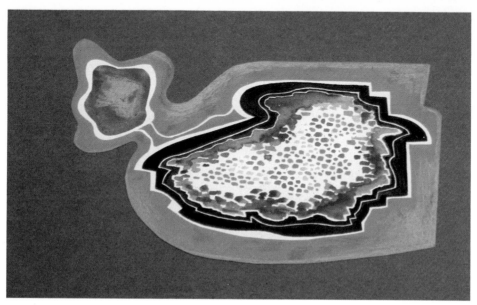

Here's something new that I call *recomposables*—three-dimensional elements that can be arranged, changed and rearranged.

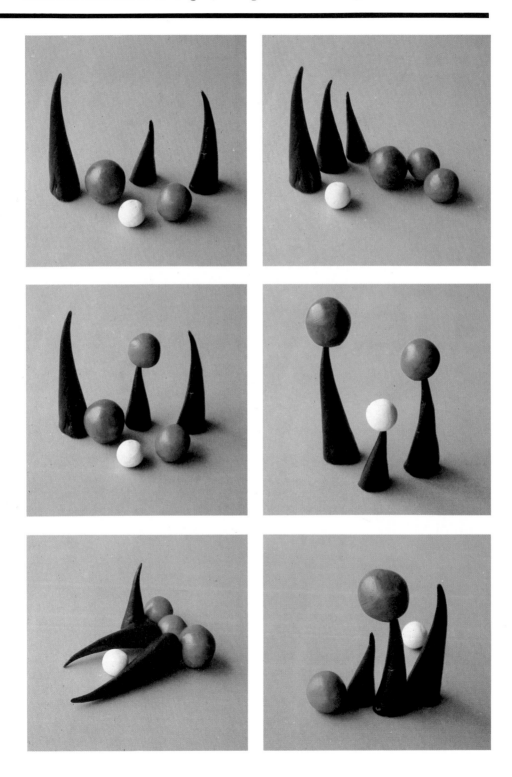

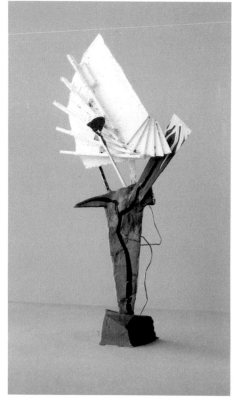

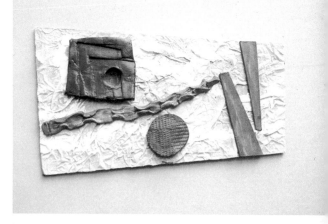

Create separate items that can be set up differently whenever the mood moves you. Perhaps a constantly changeable centerpiece, wall arrangement or mobile.

Collage

Abstract art is that form "which makes no attempt to create familiar or recognizable objects." We can, however, take pieces of already recognizable material and apply them as elements in a pleasing visual arrangement, much as we did with dots, lines and shapes.

The resulting work is a collage.

Incidentally, it might be objectively worthwhile to regard your work, or the works of other contemporary artists, as wall hangings or wall ornaments. Replacing the description "picture" or "painting" with the less conventional "dramatic wall hanging," "amusing wall ornament," etc. encourages a fresh, objective point of view.

Creating a collage offers some unusual challenges, not the least of which is the limitation imposed by the material used.

Here are some examples. Remember, their purpose is to encourage you to come up with your own creations.

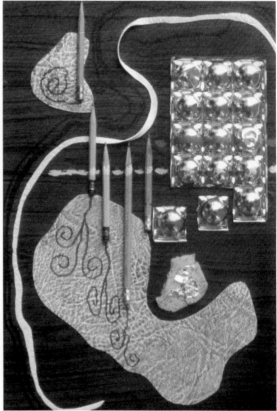

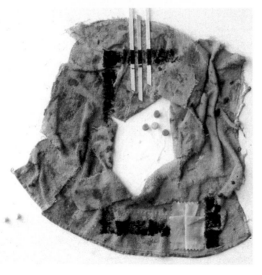

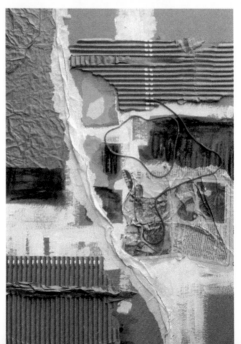

An Eye-opening Thought . . .

WORTHWHILE DESIGN IS EVERYWHERE

If you were blind and were suddenly given the ability to see, then anything visible would be magnificently worth seeing. There are scenes that can evoke unpleasant memory associations, but you can *choose* to see only the satisfying abstract design and color in any view.

To see or not to see, it's your choice!

See? . . .

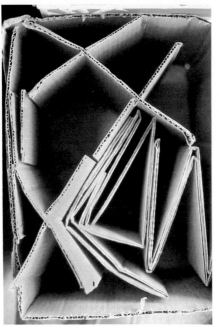

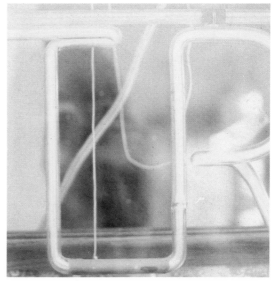

44

Robert Hasloecher

How about gathering a group together for the purposes of friendship, sharing good music, conversation *and* creating a mutual painting? A painting party! Provide, in a protected place, a large canvas illustration board or other painting surface, as well as paints, brushes, rags and media solution. Whether the painting contributions are made in order, at random, alphabetically or as a game reward, the result should in the very least be interesting, worth keeping on display if only as a memento. Usually the result is most satisfying.

How about a group graffiti or doodle composition? Hang a clean
board on a convenient wall along with hanging felt-tipped pens,
crayons, etc., and encourage family and friends to contribute their
graphic inspiration. After a week or a month or a year, frame,
hang and enjoy.

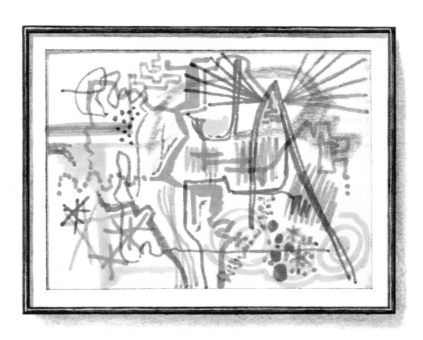

How about, with permission of the building owner, of course, paint a group abstract mural on the side of a barn?

How about, again with permission, paint a group abstract mural on a brick wall in the city?

But we don't live in an abstract world! That being the case, the following pages contain some suggestions for the practical application of abstract art.

Is that a little like suggesting that we add the unreal to the real? A better analogy would be that we are adding the "extra" to the "ordinary" or, perhaps, the "magic" to the "mundane."

So, look! Use! And find other areas where you can apply your own unique creativity.

Stitchery . . .

Elke Brengard

Mary Vahanian Anselmo

Gina Mascia

Elke Brengard

51

Pottery, jewelry . . .

Phyllis Sullivan

Josephine Glazebrook

The Acklers

Trish Van Dina

Josephine Glazebrook

The Acklers

The Acklers

Trish Van Dina

Trish Van Dina

53

Home things, flower arrangement, sails . . .

Marian Mintzer

Stained Glass Workshop/Jerry Fotinatos

Jessica Loomer

Trish Van Dina

Trish Van Dina

Ed Sheridan

Elke Brengard

Jessica Loomer

55

Lisa Thomson

Elke Brengard

. . . even pizza!

Abstract art is a form of visual poetry. Abstract art is visual music. It can shock, soothe, irritate or titillate. It can prod our emotions. It is an imagination stimulator.

A century ago photography began to undermine much of the function and purpose of the artist of that day. He began to experiment, to search for other uses for his talents than the pictorial representation of reality. No longer needed as a direct reporter of reality, he became its interpreter, its extender and distorter. He created new standards of beauty, different standards, opposite standards, the purposeful acceptance of the outrageous, anti-standards.

Today there are no universally accepted standards of beauty. Anything goes!

And this is all to the good . . . if we permit it to be. As with the optimist who says the glass is half full, opposed to the pessimist who says it is half empty, we can choose to say the lack of absolute standards of beauty is a good thing because our eyes have been opened more fully to see beauty in so many new ways rather than closed for lack of agreed-upon standards.

An abstract painting by Franz Kline, Jackson Pollock, Mark Rothko or you or, as in an experiment some years ago, the paint smears of a chimpanzee—each is a unique communication from that individual. And isn't it possible that for some, the chimpanzee's work will more pleasantly prod their emotions or excitingly stir up their imaginations?

With this in mind, and going beyond abstract art, you can consider everything you see as an arrangement of dots, lines and/or shapes. If nothing else, from now on you will, I hope, be able to see the world around you with a new point of view, with the attitude that anything you look at, since it is just an arrangement of dots, lines and/or shapes, has a positive attractive value . . . by your willful choice.

Place an imaginary frame around any object or area, and if you simply consider what you see as an arrangement of forms, colors, patterns, etc., it becomes your decision whether what you see is interesting or not. Given that choice, why not go for interesting?

The idea is that literally anything you see is at least interesting to look at. If you can accept that, you can extend yourself to the point of feeling that anything seen can be more than just interesting—it can be fascinating, can be beautiful!

This is not to say that as long as your eyes are opened you should be bombarded by constant, relentless beauty. It *does* say that at a given restful moment, when there are no unpleasant smells or sounds or other physical or intellectual distractions to disturb you, you can choose to look anywhere and be fascinated, pleased and possibly stirred.

Taste, after all, is a matter of taste!

TWO COLOR-WHEEL THEORIES

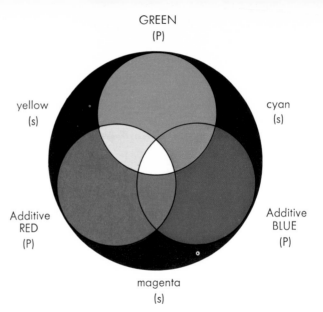

GREEN
(P)

yellow
(s)

cyan
(s)

Additive
RED
(P)

Additive
BLUE
(P)

magenta
(s)

THE ADDITIVE PRIMARIES (The Color Wheel of Light)

When two beams of colored light are projected at the same portion
of a white screen, the result is an additive mixture of light. When
light beams of green and red are mixed the result is yellow. Green and
blue produce cyan, a slighty greenish blue. Red and blue light produce
magenta, a slightly bluish red. When beams of red, green and blue are
combined, there has been a sufficient addition to create white light. White
light represents the inclusion of all colors. Red, green and blue are the
additive (light) primaries. All other colors are combined from
these primaries.

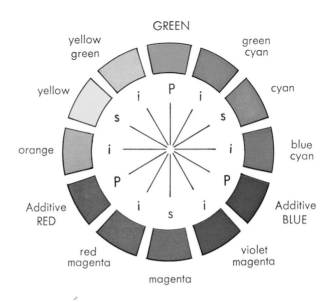

GREEN

yellow
green

green
cyan

yellow

cyan

orange

blue
cyan

Additive
RED

Additive
BLUE

red
magenta

violet
magenta

magenta

P.   Primary
s.   Secondary
i.   Intermediate

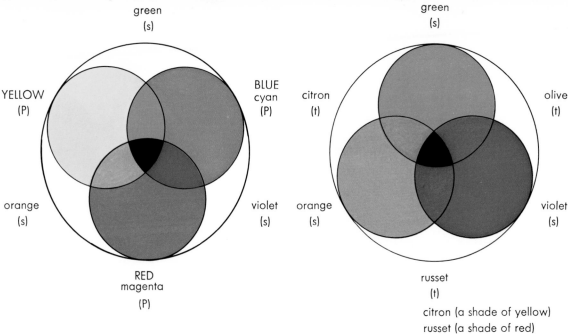

citron (a shade of yellow)
russet (a shade of red)
olive (a shade of blue)

THE SUBTRACTIVE PRIMARIES (The Color Wheel of Pigments)

When pigments (paints, inks, etc.) of different colors are mixed, the amount of visible light is reduced or "subtracted." If we mix yellow and cyan (greenish blue) pigments on a white surface, the result is green. Cyan and magenta (bluish red) produce violet. Yellow and a small amount of magenta produce orange.

When all three, magenta, yellow and cyan, are equally mixed, so much light is subtracted that the result is close to black. Black indicates the absence of all color.

Magenta (a red pigment), cyan (a blue pigment) and yellow pigment are the subtractive primaries. When using pigments, all other colors derive from these primaries.

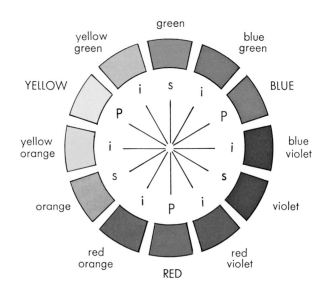

Coincidentally, these colors, which serve best as the primaries when using pigments, appear to be the same colors as those that result when we mix pairs of the primary colors of projected light.

P. Primary
s. Secondary
i. Intermediate
t. Tertiary

SOME COLOR RELATIONSHIPS OR HARMONIES

Adding white or light to a color results in a tint of that color.

Subtracting light or adding black to a color results in a shade of that color.

Adding gray (black and white) to a color mutes that color.

A shade background appears to brighten the surrounded color.

A tint background appears to mute the surrounded color.

Colors directly opposite each other on a color wheel are called *complementaries*. These are colors in greatest contrast to one another, particularly on the additive color wheel.

The combination of a color and the two adjoining that color's complement is called a *split complementary harmony*, or *relationship*.

Any three equidistant colors on a color wheel make up a *triad harmony*.

The combination of a color and those immediately adjoining it on a color wheel is called an *analogous harmony*.

Any one color and any of its tints and/or shades, ranging from white to black, comprise a *monochromatic harmony*.

There are limitless other unnamed combinations and any of these may suit your particular need. Have pleasure experimenting!

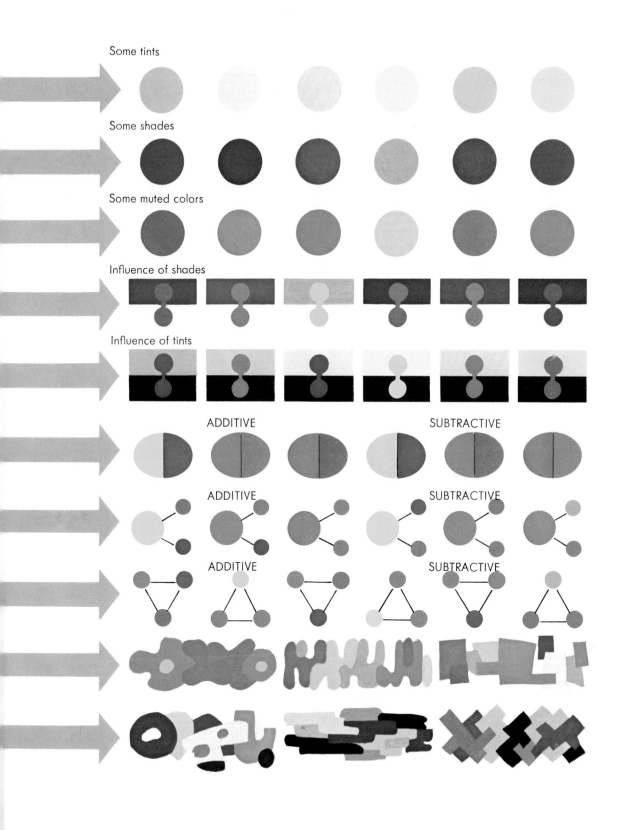

Some tints

Some shades

Some muted colors

Influence of shades

Influence of tints

ADDITIVE   SUBTRACTIVE

ADDITIVE   SUBTRACTIVE

ADDITIVE   SUBTRACTIVE